A Blue Jay Is Hungry

By Nick Vakalopoulos

Briley & Baxter Publications | Plymouth, Massachusetts

Hardcover ISBN: 978-1-961978-23-2
Paperback ISBN: 978-1-961978-24-9

Book Design: Stacy Padula

Dedication

To the First Author, Artist,
and Designer of all Creation

To My Family and Friends

A Blue Jay is hungry and looking for something.

Its tummy is empty, but there are morsels aplenty.

It flies to a tree branch and lands with a proud stance.

It looks at the ground for some food to be found.

A nut or a seed would be good indeed!

The target now acquired; the Blue Jay is inspired.

Locked on and all ready, its gaze is so steady.

The prize just below looks good don't you know?

It launches in the air without a fear or a care.

Gravity takes a hold—the Blue Jay is so bold!

Arrow like form in a wind that blows warm.

In freefall, in flight, there is such delight!

No wings needed yet; the ground shall soon be met.

Its wings now deployed; dinner will be enjoyed.

Arrival is sweet!

Now it's time to eat!

Full belly and happy, it's time to depart.

I'll remember you Blue Jay, so dear in my heart!

About the Author

Blue Jays are curious and bold by nature. They are also extremely intelligent. Watching them long enough, one can almost see the little wheels spinning in their heads as they process the world around them!

As a wildlife photographer, my goal was to capture Blue Jays in action as they went about their daily activities. One amazing observation I wanted to highlight is how Blue Jays dive to the ground from a tree branch. Essentially, they look like an arrow or missile launching into the air. They keep their wings tucked in until the very last second before they meet the earth, and it is truly a spectacular sight to behold! I wanted to showcase this amazing capability along with many other actions of Blue Jays with the images found in this book.

As with my other publication titled *There's Something About ROBINS*, all of the photographs featured within the book have been processed through a mild computer art filter, which imparts a slight illustrative quality to each picture. I am constantly inspirited and entertained by the abilities and habits of the animals I observe in the wild. There are so many unique gifts and talents bestowed upon them by their Creator. It is my hope I may have prompted each reader into a deeper reflection and appreciation of all living things in nature and the world around us.